Contents

Mandirs around the world

A **mandir** is a place where Hindus worship God. It can be a large building or a small shrine in a home. There are mandirs all over the world.

◁This mandir is in India.

This is the symbol used
to represent the Hindu faith.

For Mishka, Lasya and Tula Nansi

© 1998 Franklin Watts
96 Leonard Street
London
EC2A 4RH

Franklin Watts Australia
14 Mars Road
Lane Cove
NSW 2066

ISBN 0 7496 3154 6

Dewey Decimal Classification Number 294.5

A CIP Catalogue record for this book is available from
the British Library

Editor: Samantha Armstrong
Series Designer: Kirstie Billingham
Illustrator: Gemini Patel
Religious Education Consultant: Margaret Barratt, Religious Education Teacher Advisor
Religious Advisors: Shree Vishwa Mandir, Southall
Reading Consultant: Prue Goodwin, Reading and Language Information Centre, Reading

Printed in Hong Kong

Hindu
Mandir

Angela Wood

W

FRANKLIN WATTS

NEW YORK • LONDON • SYDNEY

Most Hindu people worship God in their home. Worship is called **puja**.

▽ The statues behind the patterned gates are of different ways of showing God.

Hindus believe in one God. They say that God can be seen in a person or an animal. Inside a mandir are statues or pictures called **murtis.** Each murti shows a different way to think about God.

7

Going to a mandir

When Hindus visit a mandir they always take off their shoes and leave them outside. This is to show their **respect** for the murtis.

They begin by ringing a bell. It's like knocking at the door to tell someone that you're there to see them.

Making an offering

Many Hindus have a murti in the mandir that is special for them. They show their love for God by bringing something to offer it. It may be water, food, **incense** or a lit flame.

▲ Sometimes people put money in an offering box.

This woman is pouring ▷ milk over the murti as an offering.

Ganesh

Most mandirs have a murti of **Ganesh**.
Ganesh has an elephant's head and a man's body.
Hindus worship Ganesh when they begin
their prayers or start something new.

◀The tiny mouse
at Ganesh's feet is
not afraid because,
although he is big,
Ganesh is very gentle.
He brings good luck.
Hindus have offered
coins to this murti
of Ganesh.

Vishnu

This murti is of **Vishnu.** He can take many different animal or human forms. Vishnu helps when things go wrong.

Krishna and Radha

In this murti, Vishnu is **Krishna**.
One story of Krishna says that he played
his flute for **gopis**, the young women who
looked after cows. He was always kind
to cows and could find them when they
got lost.

Hindus respect cows for being especially good.
This is because they produce enough milk
for everyone, and not just their own calves.

◁Krishna, playing his flute,
with a cow.

Here Krishna is with ▷
his favourite gopi, his
partner, Radha.

12

Rama, Sita, Lakshman

In many mandirs there is a murti of Vishnu as **Rama**. One day a wicked ruler sent Rama and his wife, Sita, away from their kingdom. Rama's brother, Lakshman, went with them. On their travels, a **demon** called Ravana kidnapped Sita. The monkey god Hanuman helped Rama to save Sita.

Rama is in the ▷ middle, Sita on the right and Lakshman on the left. Hanuman is in front, worshipping Rama and Sita. Rama and Lakshman always carry bows and arrows to fight off evil.

and Hanuman

Hanuman was a true friend to Rama, Sita and Lakshman.

◀A painting of Ravana, the ten-headed demon, made by children in a Hindu school.

This murti is of Hanuman. ▶

15

Shiva

Shiva destroys bad things such as wars and diseases. Shiva is also the Lord of time.
He has three eyes so that he can look at the past, the present and the future.
He has a three pronged stick to show that he is beating evil.

Shiva has a river flowing through ▷ his hair. Hindus say it is the river of life, the Ganges. It flows from heaven, through his hair, to earth.

16

A school at the mandir

Some mandirs have a school where children can learn about Hindu stories and festivals. They see how to live a Hindu life and they can work and play with other Hindu children.

Like most Hindu women, their teacher Rani wears a **sari** with a short blouse. A sari is a long, straight piece of cloth. A Hindu woman winds one end of the sari round her waist, makes some pleats at the front and tucks them in. Then she brings the other end over her shoulder.

Hindus often have a ▷ mark of coloured powder on their forehead. It is called a tilak.

When Hindus see a murti in the mandir, they put their hands together in front of their chest and say, "Namaste!".
This means "Honour to you". Sometimes when Hindus greet a person, they do the same. They believe that God is in everybody.
They are greeting God in everyone that they meet.

When they pray in the mandir,
Hindus bow. Sometimes their foreheads
touch the ground.
This shows their love and respect for God.

Dancing in a mandir

Hindus often dance as a way of worshipping. They use their hands and body to tell a story.

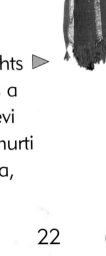

There is dancing for nine nights ▷ during Navaratri. Navaratri is a festival that honours Mahadevi or the Great Mother. In the murti above, she is shown as Durga, a strong, energetic woman.

22

Every day at the mandir there is a ceremony called **arti.** One person moves an arti lamp in front of a murti. The people in the mandir pass their hands over the flame and over their foreheads and hair.

Because the lamp has been passed in front of the murti, they feel they have a blessing from God. At the same time, everyone else sings prayers.

An arti lamp has five flames ▷ because we have five senses. It also stands for air, earth, fire, water and space.

Music in a mandir

In a mandir, there is often music. Hindu people gather together to sing in a special way called a **chant**. They play instruments that come from India such as bells, a drum and a tambourine.

Some songs last a long time.
They are poems set to music,
telling stories of God.
The drums and bells beat the
rhythm of the music and make
it easy to clap and join in.

Sometimes a few
words are chanted
over and over.

Prashad

When Hindus leave the mandir,
they are given **prashad**.
Prashad is food that has been
offered to God.

Prashad is usually sweets,
nuts or fruit. It is never meat because
most Hindus do not eat meat.

Here the pandit ▷
is giving out water
and prashad.

Glossary

arti   a ceremony using light, usually five flames

chant   a repetitive song

demon   an evil spirit

Durga   God seen as a woman who is strong and powerful

Ganesh   God seen as a man with an elephant's head

gopi   a young woman who looks after cows

incense   perfumed smoke

Krishna   God seen as a baby, child and young man

mandir   a place where Hindus worship

murtis   statues or pictures to show God

pandit	a Hindu priest
prashad	food that is offered to murtis and shared with everyone visiting the mandir
prayers	the words people say to God
puja	the Hindu word for worship
Radha	Krishna's partner. Radha was a gopi
Rama	God seen as a young prince
respect	to treat well
sari	a long, straight piece of cloth worn by Hindu women
Shiva	God seen as a man who destroys evil
Vishnu	God seen as a man who helps when things go wrong

Index

Photographic acknowledgements:
Cover: Steve Shott Photography.
P6. Sonia Halliday Photography.
P7 Top: Circa. P22. Right: Trip.

All other photographs are by Steve Shott Photography.

With thanks to the Shree Vishwa Mandir, Southall, the Bhaktivedanta Manor, Hertfordshire and Suriacumar, Rekha and Khiloni Meggi.